99 WAYS TO
MAKE A PIPE

Proble[...]mokers

Brett Stern

Library of Congress Cataloging-in-Publication Data available.

ISBN: 978-0-9834917-8-1

Manufactured in Canada.

Designed by Alan Dubinsky.

Overcup Press
4207 SE Woodstock Blvd. #253
Portland, OR 97206
Overcupbooks.com

DISCLAIMER: FOR ADULTS ONLY.

This book features pictures of methods for smoking cannabis that are illegal under federal law as well as the laws of certain states, but also legal for medical and/or recreational use in other states. All content depicted in this book is intended for adults over the age of twenty-one (21) and is for entertainment purposes only. Readers should not attempt to imitate the methods of smoking cannabis depicted herein without employing personal judgment and common sense. Overcup Press, LLC, and the author, Brett Stern, make no representations or warranties as to the safety or efficacy of the methods for smoking cannabis as depicted in this book and readers do so at their own risk. Further, Overcup Press, LLC and the author, Brett Stern, expressly disclaim any and all liability, loss, or risk for damages, arrests and/or incarcerations, losses and/or injuries (including death) incurred as a consequence of, or directly or indirectly related to, the use or imitation of the images and verbiage contained within this book.

Ceci n'est pas une pipe.

René Magritte

INTRODUCTION

Four things place humans higher than animals on the food chain: we have opposable thumbs, we make tools, we grow and harvest plants, and we cover our bodies to protect ourselves from the environment. This book will demonstrate the first three of these attributes by using our hands to make a functional tool used to smoke something we grew. As far as the clothing part, that's optional.

I bring a unique skill set to this project. I was trained as an industrial designer, so I invent and design consumer products for a living. I have also been making ceramics my whole life. These two practices have taught me about natural and synthetic materials, how to manipulate them into something functional, and how to mass-produce them, whether it's a surgical instrument or a potato chip. Some of this I learned in college. My sophomore year I had a project that involved using 2" clear plastic tubing and a full workshop at my disposal. With the leftover materials I built my first bong. So yes, I actually did study pipe making in college.

This exercise is all about embracing your creativity to solve problems; specifically, the problem of having cannabis flower but no pipe. I'd argue that if we open our eyes and minds wide enough to what's in our immediate environment there are always many solutions. As the title suggests, this book offers 99 ways to solve that problem. However, the subject of pipe building is really just a clever way to demonstrate your own problem solving potential. Hopefully, it encourages you to explore and invent new solutions to all of life's problems, not just this one. And, if you can up-cycle some junk into something more useful, you win!

INTRODUCTION

When choosing an object to fashion into a pipe, the first thing to consider is the composition of the base materials: what is it made from? I suggest using metal, wood, ceramic, or glass materials. Most raw and manufactured foods work well too. Don't use anything that will burn or melt, **and most importantly, never use anything that could become toxic when you light up.** Remember, you will be inhaling the smoke.

Everything included here was accomplished with tools that I have in my toolbox. As a craftsperson, I'll admit that I have a large toolbox. However, you can create most of the pipes described in the book with things you probably have around the house: kitchen knives, scissors, chop sticks, wooden skewers, hammers, utility knives, nail files, rubber bands and of course duct tape. If you want to up your game, a cordless drill with a several drill bits wouldn't hurt.

Note: the title of this book is *99 Ways To Make A Pipe*, NOT, 99 Ways To Make Fire. Having a lighter, match, flint stone, or magnifying glass is on you.

Here are some other pro-tips:

- Safety first. Before trying anything in this book use a good deal of personal judgment and common sense.
- DO NOT use anything plastic that will come into direct contact with a flame.
- DO NOT put a flame near anything that has a painted or printed surface.
- DO NOT use anything that has a lubricant on the surface.

- DO NOT inhale if it doesn't smell like pot burning.

- Sand off any clear finishes applied to wood surfaces.

- Remove any internal plastic or rubber parts before lighting up.

- Wash all surfaces with soap and water prior to putting it in your mouth, including that apple.

- When needed, wear a dust mask.

- Open the windows to get some fresh air throughout the entire process of making a pipe and smoking with it.

The great inventor Thomas Edison was correct when he said: "Genius is 1% inspiration and 99% perspiration." Some pipes might not work the first time, but don't get discouraged. Consider it a learning process. Edison also said: "I've not failed. I've just found 10,000 ways that won't work."

Luckily for you, all the methods shown here work.

To accompany each method, I've instituted a skill-rating system indicating the degree of difficulty.

I wish you luck and happy pot smoking!

This is a pipe.

Brett Stern

1. An apple a day keeps the doctor away.
2. Find a pointy tool to carve out a bowl on the top.
3. Punch a hole in the side to connect openings.
4. Pack the bowl and smoke.

1. Time to celebrate with some champagne and cannabis.
2. Remove the foil wrapper, wrap 2/3 of the foil around a pencil and make a bowl with the last 1/3.
3. Pack the bowl, but don't smoke it yet.
4. Open the champagne and pour.
5. Make a toast and clink glasses.
6. Now you can drink and smoke.

1. Take a long walk on a beach.
2. Think about things.
3. Pick up some shells.
4. Use a nail file to sand off the ends of a shell for a mouth piece.
5. Pack the shell and smoke.
6. Think about more things.

1. Time to water the lawn.
2. Decide it would be more enjoyable if you were high.
3. Remove spray handle from hose and dry off surfaces.
4. Remove washers and any plastic parts in the nozzle.
5. Pack the bowl and smoke.
6. Enjoy all the green grass you've grown.

1. Buy a box of ten cream cakes.
2. Unwrap one and take a bite about 3/4″ off the end.
3. Tunnel out the cream filling and eat it.
4. Carve out a bowl on the top to connect with the tunnel inside.
5. Pack the bowl and smoke.
6. Remember, you still have nine more cream cakes left.

1. Make some espresso to get the morning buzz going.
2. Clean out the coffee grounds and use the funnel as a bowl.
3. Pack the bowl, smoke, and drink espresso.
4. Smoke.
5. Enjoy both buzzes.

1. Glue three or four blocks together using non-toxic glue.
2. Drill a 1/4" hole lengthwise, a 1/2" hole for a bowl, and connect the two.
3. Pack the bowl and smoke.
4. Keep playing with blocks.

1. Cut a hole in the end of tube
2. Make a screen from a piece of foil.
3. Pack the bowl and smoke.

1. Sometimes an object designed for one function is actually multifunctional.

2. Pack the bowl and smoke.

1. Find a 2x4 that isn't holding anything up.
2. Cut off a piece and drill holes to make a pipe.
3. Pack the bowl and smoke.

1. Use a pointy tool to carve a bowl on top and create a smoking hole on the front edge.
2. Tunnel through the doughy center to connect the bowl and hole.
3. Pack the bowl and smoke.
4. Smear some cream cheese on it and have breakfast.

1. Find a blank page at the end (without ink), tear out, and trim to size.
2. Roll yourself joint and smoke it.
3. Read Genesis 9:3: "Just as I gave you the green plants, I now give you everything."
4. Enjoy and praise everything natural!

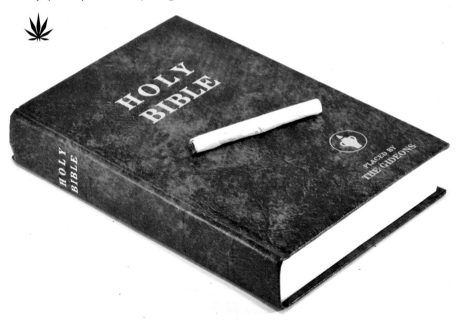

1. Throw chew toy to your best friend.
2. Get the toy back, pack the bowl and smoke.
3. Throw chew toy to your best friend.
4. Get the toy back, pack the bowl and smoke.
5. Throw chew toy to your best friend.
6. This can go on forever.

1. Cut a 1″ piece off one end and scrape out any of the fruit to make a bowl.
2. Snip off the bottom of the bowl and insert in the middle of banana.
3. Insert a chopstick through the fruit to connect with the bowl.
4. Pack the bowl and smoke.
5. Do not smoke the peel.

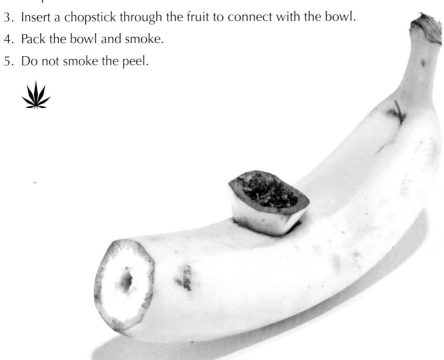

1. Pack the bowl where the balloon attaches.
2. Smoke.
3. Exhale into the balloon and pass to a friend.
4. You have just doubled the amount of weed you have by recycling.

1. Cut off a 6″ length to make pipe.
2. Make an angled cut about 1″ above the knuckle for a bowl and drill a hole in the knuckle.
3. Make your favorite tiki cocktail.
4. Pack the bowl and smoke.

1. Find any two hollow things and just tape them together.
2. Fashion yourself a screen.
3. Pack the bowl and smoke.

1. Draw yourself a hot bath.
2. Light some candles and incense.
3. Unscrew the bathtub spout.
4. Pack the very large bowl and smoke.
5. Relax and enjoy your bath.

1. Rip the top off of the wrapper and pull the straw out partway.
2. Grind up some flower and funnel down the straw.
3. Fill it as long as you want your joint to be.
4. Remove the straw.
5. Twist the top and bottom of wrapper.
6. Light the joint and smoke it.

20 | BICYCLE HANDLEBAR

1. Remove end caps from the handlebars.
2. Insert a screen into one end.
3. Pack the bowl and smoke.
4. This can be done with the handlebars on the bike, so be careful riding.

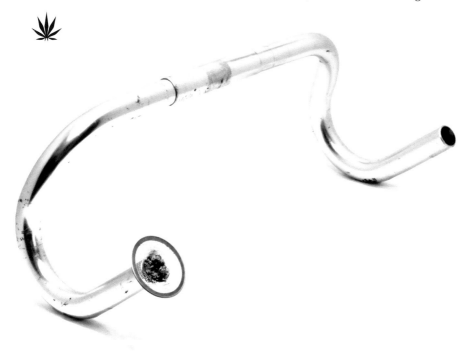

1. Ring the bell to get everyone's attention: It's 4:20!
2. Attach a brass elbow/stem plumbing fittings.
3. Pack and smoke.

1. Remove the rubber bulb from the horn.
2. Stuff a screen down into the horn.
3. Pack the bowl and smoke.
4. Return bulb to horn.
5. Always wear your helmet.

1. Get your bowling ball out of the closet.
2. Drill a 3/8" hole at an angle through one of the finger holes to connect to the thumb hole.
3. Insert a rubber stopper with a stem and bowl.
4. Insert a metal stem through the finger hole to connect with the thumb hole.
5. Pack the bowling ball bowl and smoke.
6. Now you're ready to throw some strikes.

1. Find a solid (paver) brick.
2. Drill down from the edge using a 3/8", long masonry bit.
3. Drill down to connect holes using a 1/2" masonry bit.
4. Wash out the dust.
5. Pack the bowl and smoke.
6. Gently pass the brick to your friends.
7. Brick pipe can also hold door open to get some fresh air.

1. Pull out the box of bricks.
2. Create a structure that has a chamber for stem, bowl and mouth opening.
3. Pack the bowl and smoke.
4. Admire your creation.

1. Remove the exhale valve at the base of the mask.
2. Insert a 1″ electrical conduit elbow fitting.
3. Pack the bowl and smoke.
4. Breath 100% purified air.

1. Get a pack of candy chews.
2. Lick the end of each candy and squish them together.
3. Pierce the body of the pipe with a skewer.
4. Form a bowl in the top and use the skewer to connect with the body.
5. Pack the bowl and smoke.

28 | CAR LIGHTER

1. The outlet in your car that charges phones used to be a cigarette lighter.
2. Push in the lighter to heat it up.
3. When it pops out, the element will be red hot.
4. Drop some flower on the element and it will immediately combust.
5. Breath in.
6. Don't drive!

1. Eat a carrot until you have about a 3″ length left.
2. Core out the center and carve a bowl on top using a small pocket-knife.
3. Pack the carrot and smoke.

1. Fill a watering can with water.
2. Insert a brass hose nozzle with washer into watering can opening.
3. Pack the bowl and smoke.
4. Water the plants.

1. Begin knitting a sweater using a pair of #13/10″ aluminum needles.
2. Realize getting high would improve the process.
3. Remove the end-cap and break the needle in half by bending over the edge of a table.
4. Pack the one-hitter and smoke it.
5. Keep on knitting.

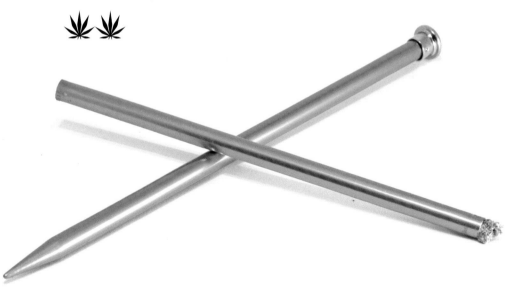

1. You're stranded on a deserted island.
2. You have an unlimited supply of coconuts.
3. Hopefully, you have an unlimited supply of flower!

1. Remove the handle from one end of the rope.
2. Pack the bowl and smoke.
3. Don't try jumping rope at this time.

1. This pipe has been staring at you forever.
2. Open the door and reach down to remove door spring.
3. Pack the bowl and smoke.

1. Remove the stick to reveal a hollow chamber in the hotdog.
2. Using the stick, carve out a bowl and connect it to the chamber.
3. Pack the bowl and smoke.
4. Eat the corndog.

1. Open your toolbox and see that your hammer has a perfect ash handle to make a pipe.
2. Drill a hole in the base and shaft to form a pipe.
3. Pack the bowl and smoke.
4. Try to hit the nail on its head.

1. Nine holes.
2. Nine one-hits.
3. Nine tee shots.
4. Nine mulligans.

1. Put flower in one end.
2. Suck through the other end.

1. Remove the wrapper so the paper keeps its tubular shape.
2. Fill with flower and smoke.
3. Keep coloring outside the lines.

1. Time to share some nectar.
2. Drill out two flower spouts and screw a bowl into one hole.
3. Fill the jar halfway with liquid.
4. Insert tubing in the other hole and up into the glass jar above the liquid.
5. Pack the bowl and smoke.
6. Remember to hang out for the hummingbirds.

1. Pour yourself a drink.
2. Remove the pourer from the bottle.
3. Pack the spout and smoke it.
4. Replace the pourer so you are ready for the next round.

1. Find a set of dominoes made from wood or stone.
2. Before playing, make a pipe from tiles and rubber bands as shown.
3. Pack the bowl and smoke.
4. Now, throw down those tiles with conviction.

1. Open up the socket set and take out the largest sockets.
2. Pack the bowls and smoke.

1. Empty the honey bear and cut off its nose.

2. Fashion a screen from a piece of foil and form around the top.

3. Pack the bowl and smoke out of honey bear's nose.

1. Staple the final report together.
2. Realize you forgot to include a chart and unstaple.
3. Insert the document and restaple the report.
4. Squeeze staple remover closed and pack the pipe.
5. Smoke.
6. Feel good that you finished your report.

1. Push a metal tube through the air valve.
2. Fill the cup with water to make a bong.
3. Pack the bowl and smoke.

1. Put one scoop of your favorite flavor in a cone.
2. Carve a bowl through the ice cream.
3. Bite the bottom off the cone.
4. Pack the bowl, smoke, and eat the ice cream.

1. Make yourself a nice cup of tea.
2. Empty the infuser and dry it.
3. Use alternative "tea" to fill the infuser.
4. Hold flame under infuser and inhale.
5. Enjoy both teas.

1. There's always an empty roll of toilet paper.
2. Cut a hole in one end of the tube and form a bowl out of foil.
3. Pack the bowl and smoke.
4. Remember to get more toilet paper.

1. Sit around a campfire and stare at the flames.
2. Carve a pipe from your pile of wood.
3. Stick a twig in the flames and light your pipe.
4. Smoke and continue to stare at the flames.

1. Place a few sucking candies in the microwave for 30 seconds.
2. Remove from microwave and roll together in a ball. Careful: they may be hot.
3. Mold the candy around a chopstick to form a pipe and bowl.
4. Remove the chopstick.
5. Pack the bowl and smoke.
6. The best part is you can suck on the pipe when you get cotton mouth.

1. Remove the set-screw from a doorknob to form a bowl.
2. Attach a metal stem if necessary, like this part from a lamp.
3. Pack the bowl and smoke.

1. Lie on the couch and see a perfect pipe in the chandelier.
2. Turn off the electricity and take it down.
3. Take the chandelier apart and remove the wires.
4. Pack the bowl and smoke.

1. Make yourself three cups of coffee using coffee pods.
2. Remove the foil lids, filter paper, and save.
3. Cut a hole in one end and attach pods using duct tape as shown.
4. Punch holes in a foil lid to create a screen.
5. Pack the bowl and smoke.
6. Enjoy the smoke and coffee.

1. Remove the batteries.
2. Drill a 5/8″ hole in the body.
3. Unscrew the end-cap and remove the spring and spare bulb.
4. Drill a 1/4″ hole in the end-cap.
5. Screw the end-cap in the body hole.
6. Pack the bowl and smoke.
7. Reassemble when done.
8. Your flashlight still works!

1. Find a hollow bunny; milk chocolate or dark chocolate, your preference.
2. Carefully remove the foil wrapper.
3. Press out the foil to form a sheet.
4. Wrap the foil around a pencil to form a stem.
5. With a knife, carve a hole into the bunny's nose the diameter of the foil stem.
6. Insert the stem into the bunny's nose.
7. Bite an ear off the bunny's head.
8. Pack the bowl and smoke.
9. Eat the bunny's other ear.

   Note: This will also work on chocolate Santas.

1. This T fitting even has a built-in carburetor.
2. Pack the bowl and smoke.

1. Remove a popsicle from the freezer and let it thaw for three minutes.
2. Open the bottom of the wrapper and pull the stick out of the popsicle.
3. Bite off the top 2″ of the popsicle to form a chamber.
4. Carve out a bowl in one end with the stick.
5. Pack the bowl and smoke.
6. Enjoy the icy smoke.

1. This is one of those situations where you need to decide if you can sacrifice the drink for the smoke.

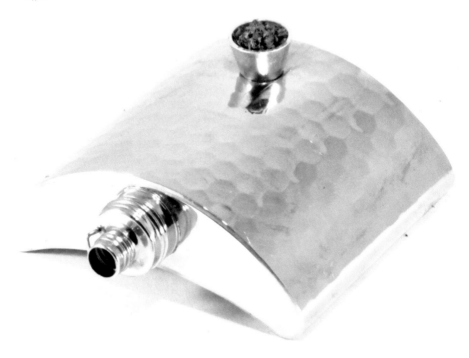

1. Do you really need instructions?

1. Wake up and start your morning routine.
2. Take out two coffee filters, some coffee, and flower.
3. While waiting for water to boil, tear apart one filter and roll a joint.
4. Pour water over coffee in the second filter.
5. Drink your coffee and smoke your joint.
6. Get your morning buzz going.

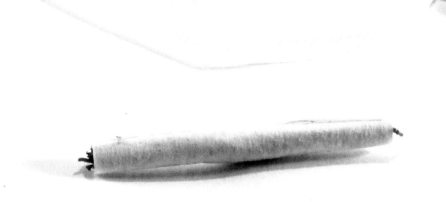

1. It's like this was designed to be a pipe.
2. Make sure there is no paint on the surface where you are lighting.
3. Pack the bowl and smoke.

1. Smoking leads to drinking.
2. Or,
3. Drinking leads to smoking

1. Play some tunes on your kazoo.
2. Unscrew the cap and remove the filter paper.
3. Pack the bowl and smoke.
4. Put the filter paper back in and play some more tunes.

1. Get a canning jar, any size will work.
2. Drill two 1/4″ holes in lid.
3. Insert one 1/4″ brass M/M connector.
4. Attach a 1″ plastic tubing length on the inside and 12″+ length on the exterior to fitting.
5. Insert one 1/4″ brass M/F connector.
6. Attach 4″ plastic tubing length on the inside.
7. Pack the bowl and smoke.

1. Get a large portabella mushroom.
2. Carve out a bowl in the stem.
3. Carve out a stem in a carrot and insert it in the mushroom stem.
4. Pack the bowl and smoke.

1. Wrap several layers of foil around a lighter to form a 6-8" tube.
2. Make a 2" incision above the flint wheel to form a bowl.
3. Pack the bowl, light the lighter, and smoke.

1. Insert a bowl into the side of a navel orange.
2. Carve a hole in the navel end of the orange.
3. Insert your finger until it touches the stem, and wiggle to create a cavity.
4. Pack the bowl and smoke.
5. Eat the orange and get your vitamin C fix.

1. Set a blank canvas on an easel.
2. Stare at the blank canvas.
3. Stare at the blank canvas.
4. Stare at the blank canvas.
5. Need inspiration.
6. Pull the metal ferrule off the paint brush.
7. Pack the bowl and smoke.
8. Get inspiration.
9. Paint your masterpiece.

1. Find a pepper, any color will do, but don't use a hot pepper.
2. Cut two holes in body.
3. Form a bowl out of foil and insert in one of the holes.
4. Pack the bowl and smoke.

1. Before you play, pack a bowl and smoke it from your paddle.
2. Focus.
3. Kill shot!

1. Take apart a broken umbrella.
2. Pack the metal pipe and smoke.
3. Go outside and enjoy the rain without an umbrella.

1. Take apart a teabag to form a sheet of rolling paper.
2. Roll a joint and smoke it.
3. Put the loose tea in an infuser and make a nice cup of tea

1. Find your favorite spud.
2. Insert your choice of metal bowls.
3. Using a skewer, make a shaft hole and connect to the stem.
4. Make sure you get good air flow.
5. Pack the bowl and smoke.

1. Now, if you could only remember where you left your keys.

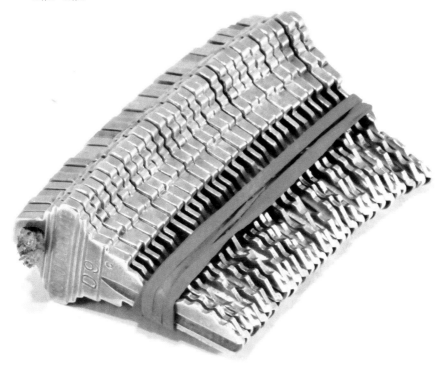

1. Smoke seven bowls and play some tunes.

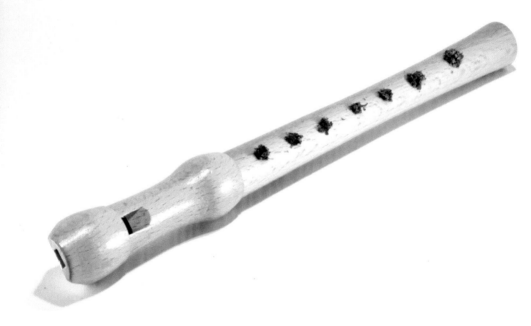

1. Decide to make your favorite pie.
2. Using the rolling pin to make some pie dough.
3. Remove handles and use pin as pipe.
4. Pack the bowl and smoke.
5. Put pie in the oven and wait.
6. Pack the bowl and smoke some more.
7. Don't forget to check the oven to see if pie is done.

1. Select your favorite salt & pepper shakers.
2. Remove the plugs and empty the spices.
3. Insert a foil bowl in the openings.
4. Pack the bowls and smoke.

1. Watch a YouTube video on how to remove a sink pop-up assembly.
2. Remove the sink pop-up assembly.
3. Pack the bowl and smoke.
4. Watch a YouTube video on how to install the part you removed.
5. Reinstall the plumbing.

1. Find an ocean to swim in.
2. Place a screen over the snorkel top.
3. Pack the bowl and smoke.
4. Jump in water and marvel at the underwater beauty.

1. Take a hammer and pound a concave shape into the sprinkler head.
2. Pack the bowl and smoke.
3. Turn on the sprinkler.

1. Remove the faucet from exterior of your house.
2. Pack the bowl and smoke.

1. Pull off the rubber stylus and the metal end-cap.
2. It's a hollow tube that is a perfect one-hitter.
3. Pack the one-hitter and smoke it.
4. You can always use your finger as a stylus.

1. Lick ten candies on each side and stick together.
2. Pack the end of the candy tube and smoke.

1. Turn-off the water main.
2. Remove the valve.
3. Pack the bowl and smoke.
4. Reinstall the valve and turn the water on.

1. Select your favorite processed meat.
2. Carve a chamber and a bowl with a skewer and connect them.
3. Check for airflow.
4. Pack the bowl and smoke.
5. Enjoy the taste of smoked cannabis and smoked meat.

1. Make a pot of tea.
2. Refill the pot with pot and more water to make teapot bong.
3. Smoke.

1. Pack everything you need for camping in the wilderness.
2. Set up your campsite.
3. Realize you forgot your pipe.
4. Remove the elastic cord from the tent poles.
5. Use the tent poles as one-hitters.
6. Enjoy camping.
7. Remember to put tent back up before it gets dark.

1. Empty the wrapper of its contents.
2. Fill the wrapper with flower and twist the ends to seal.
3. Light up a giant spliff and smoke it.

1. Cook a meal.
2. Add some cracked pepper.
3. Take apart the pepper mill.
4. Pack the bowl and smoke.

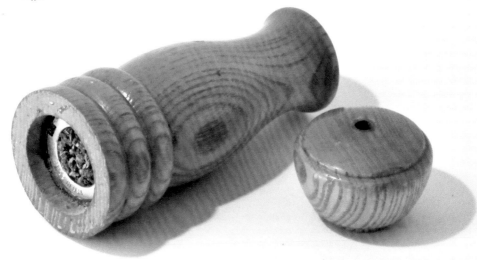

1. Unscrew the pressure gauge and remove all the parts.
2. Screw back together.
3. Pack the bowl and smoke.

1. Make the Thanksgiving turkey.
2. Invite your friends and family over to celebrate.
3. Take apart a glass or metal baster while turkey is cooling down, and form a foil bowl over end.
4. Pack the bowl and smoke.
5. Carve the turkey.
6. Be grateful for all you have.

1. You do need toilet paper.
2. You don't need the toilet paper holder.
3. Pack the bowl and smoke.

1. Drill a hole in top.
2. Insert a stem and bowl.
3. Fill the jug with water.
4. Pack the bowl and smoke.
5. Don't drink the bong water!

1. Get a 3'-6' length of cable.
2. Remove and recycle the wire.
3. Attach cable connectors to both ends.
4. Pack the bowl and smoke.

1. Cut a hole in the top of the watermelon.
2. Tunnel out the inside and carve out and air chamber.
3. Make a bowl from a carrot.
4. Cut a hole in the side and insert a straw.
5. Pack the bowl and smoke.
6. Slice open the watermelon and eat it.

1. Remove the cork ball inside the chamber.
2. Pack the bowl and smoke.
3. Get back to calling game, if you can see clearly.

1. You're sitting and can't get up at the moment.
2. Reach around and grab your plunger pipe.
3. Pack the bowl and smoke.
4. Enjoy.
5. Flush.
6. Wash hands.

1. Build a tower.
2. Take seven blocks off the top.
3. Bind together as shown using four rubber bands.
4. Pack the bowl and smoke.
5. Keep playing, being careful not to knock the tower over.
6. Focus.

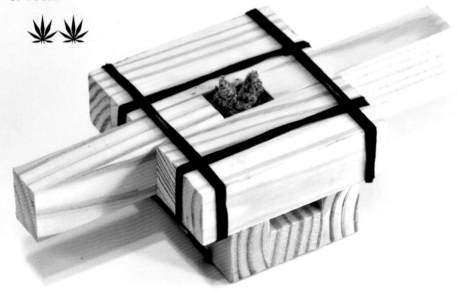

Brett Stern is an industrial designer/craftsman. He's spent his career inventing and patenting surgical instruments; Brett was the creator/founder of Beer Chips®, where he discovered how to put beer into potato chips without making them soggy; and he also makes a line of ceramic ashtrays for pot smoking that can be found at dazedandglazed.com.

Brett smokes pot and rides his bike, although not at the same time, in Portland, Oregon.

99pipes.com

Previous Books:
99 Ways to Open a Beer Bottle Without a Bottle Opener (Chronicle Books, 2015)
Inventors at Work (Apress Publishing, 2011)